For ana ... .

for
AND
against

Sharon McCartney

Edited by Ross Leckie.
Cover and interior page design by Julie Scriver.
Cover imagery: Free-Photo-Gallery.org and stock.xchng.com
Printed in Canada on 100% PCW paper.
10 9 8 7 6 5 4 3 2 1

Library and Archives Canada Cataloguing in Publication

McCartney, Sharon, 1959-
For and against / Sharon McCartney.

Poems.
ISBN 978-0-86492-539-8

I. Title.

PS8575.C427F67 2010   C811'.54   C2009-906116-3

Goose Lane Editions acknowledges the financial support of the Canada Council for the
Arts, the Government of Canada through the Book Publishing Industry Development
Program (BPIDP), and the New Brunswick Department of Wellness, Culture, and Sport
for its publishing activities.

Goose Lane Editions
Suite 330, 500 Beaverbrook Court
Fredericton, New Brunswick
CANADA E3B 5X4
www.gooselane.com

For Shane Neilson

Contents

11 Decaf

12 After Little Italy

13 A Relationship

14 The Variety of Autumn Sunrises in Fredericton

15 Recurrent Military Imagery

16 Against Sanitation

17 Ill, I Walk the Old Railbed on a Windy Day in March

18 How They Died

19 Gabriel's Peace Camp

20 Through

21 Impending Death of the Cat

22 Yield

23 Saint John River in Flood

24 Dog

25 Lady Ashley

26 Against Mussels

27 Raccoon up a Tree

28 Against Happy Stories

29 Against Form (Lake Huron)

30 Refrain

31 Against Skinny-Dipping

32 Cataract

33 Against Parallelism

34 Unqualified

35 Against Memory

36 Against Overlong Sound Checks

37 ATM

38 Dorothy

39 Risotto

40 Refuse (Against Tolstoy)

41 Abandon

42 Snow White

43 Sixteen Years Ago
44 For (Against) Judith
45 Against All That
46 Marie Antoinette's Last Thoughts
47 Tsunami, Earthquake, Hurricane
48 After Roncesvalles
49 Against Coyotes
50 Against Stagnation
51 Mrs. Oliver Mellors
52 And Now the Looting Begins
53 Against Skunks
54 Against Irony
55 Against Marriage
56 Against Scaffolding
57 Against Losing My Wallet
58 Against Therapy
59 Against Imagination
60 Fathom
61 Solitude
62 Subversion
63 For My Sister's Brain
64 Crux
65 For Fidelity
66 Against Being Convenient
67 Against Self Negation
68 For the Walker
69 For Fredericton
70 For George Eliot
71 For Alcohol
72 For the Coe Slide
73 For Pigeon Lake

75 Acknowledgements

for AND *against*

Decaf

Like donning a tiara of nails, those days when I brewed
decaf by mistake, pain in my skull, something ungraspably
awry, as if a child were suffocating in a van I couldn't open
or I woke to blue paint peeling like burnt skin, curtains in
soggy heaps, the cat moaning. I thought the end was coming.
After three days, I checked the labels, my ballpoint scrawl,
frost-faded, grabbed the right beans, Kenya AA, 18% cream
from the Mennonites, and the ice-jam of horror in my bones melted,
the skittish lights on the walking bridge winked out, the sun,
a pink fist, rose resolutely over the Irving storage facility,
transfusing the soapy Saint John. I kissed my dog on the muzzle,
puzzling him, elated, like seeing a vision of Christ in firelight
or the Virgin's tears falling from granite, synapses rewired,
all systems up — not just coffee, but redemption, the troubled
teenager relenting, asking for you, or the surgeon glancing up
from the chart, saying *no, we were wrong, it's nothing after all.*
Happiness distilled, enhanced, a dark blend of joy, like glimpsing
a handsome stranger arcing an axe under cedars, splitting stumps
into kindling, the animal exhalation each time contact is made,
the blade bites deeper, and realizing you are married to him.

After Little Italy

After too many pints of brown at the Communist's Daughter,
the bartender's muted horn, *sotto voce* undermining contentment
like a duplicitous friend, sparking friction, I'm stomping back
to the Delta, shoulder-checking leisurely Saturday summer night
amblers, tube-topped, spaghetti-strapped tourists, right and left,
you at my heels, anger on anger, petty resentments we've collected
over the years spilling out, 52 pickup, littering the sidewalk.
Actually shouting at each other on Bloor — like the couples we've
always laughed at, trailer park romance. So caught up in it, divorce
the only thing we can agree on, we lose track, forget where we are,
which way to the hotel. *We're on Yonge Street* — you stop as if
at a precipice. *I hate Yonge Street!* And I, out of habit or love,
I don't know which, pity you. That part of you I know too well,
that won't wait in line, that despises the tawdry crowd, *ordinary*
fucking people — , said Harry Dean Stanton in *Repo Man*. Later,
in our room, a *Seinfeld* rerun, wordless reconciliation. You're
a little bewildered; first, I want out, then, I want sex. Forget
what I said. I was hammered, my thoughts a jumble of elbows,
desire, regret, bumping rudely on a street you never wanted to see.

A Relationship

Though the old cat both fears and detests
the dog, she wants the warmth of the room.
The dog curled beside me on the bed, the rest
of the house unheated. She hooks a claw
under the door, then thins herself to slip
through the crack. Pauses on the rug,
staring at us, alarmed. If the dog moves,
she jumps, imagines he means harm.
But he's just preparing to leave.

The Variety of Autumn Sunrises in Fredericton

Yesterday, fog so thick it rattled audibly
in the ochre and amber maple. Today,
cloudless, still, a full moon illuminating
the turquoise hull of pre-dawn sky.
Standing outside, shivering, waiting
for the dog to crap, anchors your morning
wonderfully. Later, a walk on the green,
along the Saint John, the dog excited,
nosing the strata of leaves, mad dashes
in the muddy shallows, a dramatic leap —
he's showing off, giddy with freedom,
the chill in the air. Autumn's the best
season here, season of dying, surrender.
None of the violent urgency of spring,
icy sidewalks awash in slush, unsettling
swings in temperature. Nor the irritation
of summer, sleepless heat, enervation.
October leaves you alone, lets you be,
its attention elsewhere. Only the open
vistas of winter ahead, bare branches,
clarity, certainty, the river frozen over.

Recurrent Military Imagery

Rommel driving deep into Egypt, bulbous-
headed U-boats ping-pinging off Halifax,
bejewelled armies advancing majestically,
doomed Polish cavalry, Slavic triangular faces,
thin-skinned Shermans raising orchards of dust,
periscopes, telescopic lenses,

                   no, not military —
an overstuffed armchair, a warehouse packed
with boxes, stacks tilting, a half-ton's axles
dripping mud, a candle going down the well,
windlass moaning, *no, that must be me,*
Robert Capa and Ingrid Bergman in ruined
Berlin, Robert Jordan and Maria under pines,
don't laugh, Robert Blake and that stupid bird,
don't laugh, Heinkels, Junkers, Spitfires, air
crumpled like wrapping paper, distant tremors,
stop it —

        galloping on hard sand, dark Arkansas
highways, my head in his lap, a story so good
the walls of my room surprise me, diving, not
breathing, blue water, blue sky, pressure building,
hot Baja sun penetrating dermal layers, a guerilla,
the underground, Paris in 1944, *no,* a bottle
of Pacifico sweating on his Che beach towel.

It was like eighteen, I say afterward,
rearranging my face. *What a shame, then,*
he replies, *that I only had three.*

Against Sanitation

Antiseptic dichromatic funereal hospital smell of floral bleach,
slippered feet shuffling, the dementia in 506 hollering *help*
all night, and how I shook, how I trembled, how I laboured
with pain and fear the way I once laboured with child, marooned
at my fifth floor window, tensored, opiated, while below me, salt-
streaked school buses ground their chalky gears down college hill
toward the Nashwaaksis, young men leaned through the too-tight
curve of the Trans-Canada, everyone accelerating, glorying, as it
appeared to me, in the hegemonic ordinariness of morning, blessed
dirty rush-hour world that had been ripped from my grasp like jewellery
I had shoplifted, an awfulness of which I am unable to speak. Poison.
And that's why I say to you now and ever don't shower after old-timers
hockey, don't rinse it away, come home to me with your ignominious
armpits, your skunky rancour, truculence, your love of violence and
force, your putrid, decaying-from-the-inside leather-of-the-glove stench
of your fingers as they enter me, your fungal jockstrap, your groin pull,
back spasms, bursitis, tendinitis. Let me undress you, your KV-67s
jersey so vile, bacterial, the cat comes trotting, tail erect in adoration.
Let me lay you down, stretch you out, and taste the salt on your cock
that tastes like rain, amniotic, like being born, desire such a becoming,
an opening, your unsanitized cells in mine, organic, meiotic, benign.

Ill, I Walk the Old Railbed on a Windy Day in March

Spring flurries, the sky heavy, overcome, patches
of ice from last week's thaw napped with the cream
of fresh snow. Slipping with every third step, so
desperate, so sick of it all I don't even say *fuck*
when I fall. Feverish, fluish, sneezing and sore,
but the dog *must* get out and so I plod, blinkered
behind my hood like a cart horse, negotiating
the footing, until I glance up to glimpse a spectre,
an eight-foot Shiva of snow approaching, arms out,
columnar, marching up the corridor of evergreens,
an icy twister. The dog sits his ass down slowly,
uncertain, looks back at me, and we both pause,
passive, as the frenetic, insubstantial body bear-
hugs us, passes over and under and through
and continues on, as if sated, yet undissipating,
whirling the line. The dog shakes, shivers off
the dust of snow, disgusted, pulls to move on,
but I feel caught, frozen — why did I like it?
Arctic breath in mine, brief drama of contact,
pain like a flagellation, rejuvenating, restorative,
compared to the unrelenting ache in my throat.

How They Died

My father, last of all, in a nursing home bed, perfectly alone,
sometime between his 6:30 a.m. insulin shot and breakfast
at seven. My mother, six years earlier, in a house overcrowded
with no one's colonial furniture, after weeks of morphine,
confusion, and only, at last, when the hospice nurse scolded her,
told her it was time to go. Fifteen years before that, my sister,
thirty years old, pale and thin, brittle body curved like a spear
of eucalyptus from years of coma, in an ICU high above a palm-
treed parking lot, late summer, asphalt as soft in the sun's hard
stare as my mother's sigh of relief. Thirty-four of Hannibal's
thirty-seven elephants in the Alps. Three thousand pack horses
on the Klondike's White Pass. In the '60s, any number of counter-
revolutionary grain-eating birds, sparrows, crows, in China's
countryside. Sixteen deer (I counted them) somewhere in Colorado
the time I drove non-stop, Iowa to California, fugitive from
diminishment, from inevitability, through twilight, starlight, and
then dawn with its carcasses scattered in post-coital attitudes.

Gabriel's Peace Camp

That was just angrifying. — Gabriel Jarman

The game of "rich and poor day" didn't work,
the counsellor confides later. The rich children
woken gently in their camp cots, smiles and coos,
while the poor children were shouted, tripped
out of bed to bread crusts and water, no plates.
The rich children escorted to an exotic repast,
banana pancakes, waffles, linen and cutlery
while the poor children looked on, muttering.
No matter that at lunchtime the tables were turned —
rich became poor, poor became rich. Whoever
was poor was, at that moment, unreasonably angry.

Through

Remember the night I completely lost it?
Pouring shots in the kitchen. *To irony!*
Then dancing into bookshelves. Wasn't
it obvious I was desperate? Unhappiness
a conflagration I was attempting to douse
with thimblefuls of alcohol. Nothing gets
easier. Nothing. Winter-stunned denizens
of this hateful municipality, boot-tongues
flapping, wandering the Superstore aisles
brokenly, mouths open. No, dear 84-year-old
Margaret greeting me at the pool, no, it isn't
a fresh, crisp day. It's a truly fucked-up day,
my marriage moribund, thoughts a mutinous
rabble. Your small town pride, morality,
just more ways to get suckered, hoodwinked,
hand over your taxes. Peace, charity, warmth
like the dog's favourite ball lost under snow
until April, or the cold lump of flesh incised,
the wound cauterized with the iron of desire,
blind passion — when he wants to slap me,
but gently, I let him. My life like a party
I'm dying to leave — the wrong people came.

Impending Death of the Cat

Something's wrong with the cat, scarecrow — she wanes
gossamer thin, ghostly, her spine a prominent
span, a Golden Gate, from which her mane
of dandruffed fur hangs. Hundreds at the vet,
X-rays, blood tests — still no diagnosis.
Palpated, rehydrated, she defeats
our fears, but for how long? I fold challis,
soft wool, her stately sickbed, buy Fancy Feast,
patiently sop the hazards of vomit, clean
rugs and linens ad nauseam, ignore
the debris of death, messiness, futile routine
of food and shit. Say it: nothing will restore
her health. And yet, remark her purr, her carriage,
how she embodies the state of our marriage.

Yield

Verb and noun, to capitulate, but also earnings,
revenue — so many stacks of hay, bushels of corn,
grapes on the vine. To concede, to give way,
as in traffic, idling as the line of cars passes,
and to succumb, as to pain, to duck under a cold
shower before swimming, to gulp a bitter quaff.

To say *I can't help it — this is what I am* and out
of that briery thicket, that bramble of thorns,
downcastedness, to glean a fistful of knowledge,
self-truth, burred green fruit perhaps, unripened,
inedible, but tangible.

                    Nearly everything hurts.
To profit from that, to plant the unpalatable
in forgiving sod and spade it, almost patiently,
year after year, harvest after diminishing harvest,
despite failure, despite loss, hot withering winds,
a late frost. To toil in the surety of uncertain
returns. Not to turn away, to balk, to refuse,
but to allow, to uncover oneself wilfully in
the deluge and how out of that comes value.

Saint John River in Flood

Lift the bank's calico skirt of debris —
baubles, bric-a-brac, bottles, bags, last
winter's Christmas trees — and shake it,
a sheet snapping. Humble the bridges,
ooze over oily highways, itchy rows
of potatoes, shoo the lowlifes, ungulate
and vermin, out of their quaggy homes.
Rain-drunk, aimless rage, trespassing
illicit lawns, swelling through sewers
to pool, lolling, in that imperceptible dip
on Lansdowne, lipping the languid
sandbags staggered like bricks around
the Beaverbrook, sinking into basements,
periphrastic, unkinking from north to south —
so good to forget the seasons of abeyance,
muddy knuckles cracked and shrunken,
the older brother smugness of the sun.
Snort at the gawkers, lordly amblers
on what's left of the street, as if they're
out strolling for any purpose other than
to shake their heads, *tsk tsk*. Don't give
me that. I trashed you first, betrayed
you first — you can't hurt me.

Dog

Trembles beside me, anticipating, while
the cat licks up her meat in the corner.
Knows he has to wait, but struggles,
groaning for the gap between ever
and now. He could bolt, but won't.
I think time means to him nothing more
than the need to obey. But imagination
outloops time. Takes him there, tasting
the grease the cat leaves behind. Now,
he's salivating, his real body suckered
by unreal thoughts, leaping the chasm,
the way when I think of you pulling me
down, your hand brushing my hair, I feel
myself opening, as if you're here and
everything's okay, no one is hungry.

Lady Ashley

What stays with me now is not his ardour,
his matador's grip, but the laughter when
he paused, inside me at last, and we locked
eyes, focused — *oh it's you!* — like the moment
when you unwrap a gift, a velvety box, pure joy.

Can that be sin? Like riding an ocean swell or
cresting the loft of a binge, luxury, bending
into a limousine and if only the sun wouldn't
rise, he wouldn't pull away, concave with shame,
hunched under the hisses of the crowd. *Pobre,
pobre*, so downcast. What is he thinking
when he can't look at me?

                    I don't regret anything,
ever. Remorse requires a future, investments, pay-
offs just beyond reach. What I haven't got. What
they rifled away. Love's no more than a split
of champagne twirled in ice, the cork popped —
hurrah! — and then the effervescence.

Against Mussels

Trekking the stony spit at St. Andrews with you
and the boys, the dog obsessed, zigzagging
smells, clamshells and kelp, Fundy tide waxing
with its usual bombast. Then mussels and a glass
of wine at the Breakers and later the Scott and Zelda
Algonquin, Adirondack chairs in the sun, a pint,
another, sharp words. Doubt disinterred. Turmoil:
if *nothing happened* with the plastered young woman
you ushered home from the pub, then why was it
hard to explain? Your furious dismissal, rolling
your eyes at my loony-tunes anger. My helpless rage:
why don't you leave me? — you so obviously want to —
do us both a favour. Gather the children; they're wary,
eyes narrowed. Then, two hours home. You're taking
the curves too fast, daring me to complain, merciless,
and soon, soon, nausea begins, soon, I'm sweating,
pale, dim, puking again and again, knees gravel-pocked,
beside the fuming car. You ease up, pull over in Harvey,
my misery sparking geniality, tentative kindness.
Back on the road, gut quelled, sipping soda, I make
an effort, play Howlin' Wolf, a concession to your taste
and to the recalcitrant moon in the rearview.

Raccoon up a Tree

Nest-plunderer, lumbering garbage can cracker,
she endures daylight's incipient torpor, oncoming
ennui of midsummer heat, jeered by a mélange
of brattish crows. Suburban nuisances all, but
the raccoon is subtle, at least, unlike the ADD
assholes bobbing almost nautically from branch
to limb, belled buoys that tilt, dip, and clang,
waking the house. Slippered, robed, I'm under
the maple at 6 a.m. wondering at the racket,
while she's nestled numb in a crook, clawed toes
dangling like disjointed charms. Spoiled starlet,
the folds of her full torso wallow indulgently,
a black quilted mask pulled over her eyes. I envy
her indolence, autonomy, how little she cares
for the baiting taunts, avian unblinking stares.
She lazes out the day in shade while I come and go,
gazing up from the lawn below. With darkness,
she descends, waddles off unseen, up to no good.
Two nights later, Mark hears the spit and snarl
of savage sex, raccoons fucking in the riverbank
weeds, tells me how the sounds travelled, crossed
Waterloo, audibly urgent, disrupting his citronella
candle fugue. I imagine it was her, envy her anew.

Against Happy Stories

Faux Irish pub, synthetic timbered walls,
peanut husks ground to desiccate under boots,
but the beer's decent — oatmeal stout from Quebec,
pleasant buzz until she hoists her pint my way,
brandishing, determined to "share." *Oh shit,*
I think, *here it comes,* familiar damned tale,
how scared she was, phoning the doctor, dread
coiled in her throat, waiting, and at last the report:
all clear. A click, hang up, breathe in, and life
restarts, her fear a chimera now (*phew*). We join
to cheer, to toast her long life, her luck. I loathe
myself. Wrathful, stewing, I nod, grin, and drink,
drink, drink rather than think what I don't want
to think, how, to me, she appears to gloat, preen,
and strut. The pity — she's blameless, unaware.
How could she know? I hide the scars, never
bring up how it was like being dumped, *please
fuck off,* by the one I want more than air, the one
who romps, so nonchalant, with her in front
of me now, unabashed, insouciant, flaunting
his choice, puckered mouths, elbows locked.

Against Form (Lake Huron)

Anger, self-pity, it all burns down eventually,
the scrap wood beach fire I scrabbled away
from earlier, shins scorched, more inviting now,
past midnight, turning inward. My friends,
two couples, gone to bed, leaving me alone,
a bottle of red tilted in dirt. Brooding. Leaden
lake unmoved, drumming its fingers. Seems
like I can only define what I don't want, to be
closeted in my room upstairs, surrounded by lovers,
gritty sheets, muffled coughs behind latched
cottage doors, inevitability etched in that structure,
antiquated as it is, graceful decay, crooked pine
walls, floorboards buckled, rickety sink sinking,
nearly knee-high. My instinct to flee. Shred
strictures, expectation — my mother's subtracted
future laid out for her at twenty, a floral arrangement,
funereal tones deepening as it dried. Anything
but that. To strip in moonlight, to phosphoresce,
court randomness, scatter desire like stars,
see what befalls, pain, a life so confusing
the Surrealist after-dinner games made sense.
Oh cork the bottle. That's the end. Time to snooze,
to lay my rattled head on my hands, no pillow
but the sand, no blame to shed but my own.

Refrain

What I fail to do,
repeatedly.

Against Skinny-Dipping

Riding shotgun north of the 401, hot red rental, D & M cramped
in the rear, all of us enfolded in bucolic loveliness, teams of fat
golden Belgians harrowing vast Mennonite hayfields, chaste
women in calico setting out galvanized buckets of gladioli that
call to mind my mother *twirling before a mirror in a new dress —*
in her 60s, still wanting to please and then it dies, the good feeling,
the talk turning to getting naked, what a lark it will be, relentless,
revisiting wheres and whens, beaches, baths. I hate this. Can't
undress for anyone, every disaster torched on my body in scars.
So fucked to be that. I see what's ahead, a mixed-up weekend
of hurt, every mild sorrow tumbled at my feet like sour clothing,
looking away while three pale immortals mount the surf.

Cataract

Desire that I thought lay dormant, vanquished,
recurs with the vehemence of a river narrowing,
plunging over a precipice, *crescendo, glissando*,
as if I were backfloating in the lobe of a dark
lake and, suddenly, I'm jarred, a tug, snagged
by an invisible line, ankles bound, snugged
under the surface into obscurity, a cloudiness
that confounds — no, I'm not stupid, but I do

stupid things. Like anyone. Those daredevils
who nailed themselves into drums or barrels
and hopped the Niagara — did they hope their lives
would cohere, that the prodigal would return,
reciprocate, would love them with the clarity
that sobers the rapids but does not in any way
diminish the depths that might be fathomed
if only *oh too romantic* one could breathe

underwater? Or were they beyond caring?
Gyrating in blackness, heart rate spiking,
enthralled nevertheless by the noisy heave-ho,
the current that piggybacks them and me to
the gut-drop, hang-time of upwelling doom —
failure, rejection, divorce, whatever it was
that brought down those grisly rocks before us.

Against Parallelism

The sadness, two vectors, equidistant,
soldiering along side-by-side, in tandem,
but separate. The most microscopic gap
equals an abyss, unbridgeable. Why
doesn't one or the other veer off?

They'll never meet — no intersection,
no conjunction, no tender commingling,
fevered kisses, waking up with someone
other than the dog in one's arms, no
watching NFL with the sheets pushed
down, passing a cold beer back and forth.

They must want it this way, mirroring
each other, a refusal to be the one who
drifts even a fraction of a degree, rejecting
the imperfection of giving in to passion,
the fey waywardness that might upset
the equation, might force them to touch,
to embrace a world without parallel.

Unqualified

In those early unsettled days, Iowa City, Seattle,
it was all you — you in your cement-flecked
workboots, torn anorak, your six-pack of Coors
in a backpack slung on your burled shoulder.
I was a goner, cuckoo from the moment we met.
Ready to give up everything — California,
my mother crying on the phone — to have you.
Your Papa Hemingway beard, garish Sally Ann
shirts, untucked. Your chippiness, quick temper,
fisticuffs in the Shamrock, busting pearl buttons,
and sluttishness, fucking around (just like me).
Your indie-band enthusiasm, a form of pride —
Joy Division, Gun Club, Magazine, Siouxsie Sioux —
I wanted it all. What did I know? I was twenty-two.

Against Memory

I've had it with the past, elusive friend, would banish
it if I could, join an AA of reverie-addicts, of staring
emptily out the train window while the world rattles
by, feeling as sidetracked as abandoned flatcars.

Forget, forget. Tuck troublesome thoughts
in the back pocket of my jeans and wash them.
Forget inconstancy, untruth, forget the ripped
Velcro sound I hear in my heart when I tear
myself from those I love, forget betrayal,
forget being forgotten.

                        Until I open the dryer
and out tumbles my smudged scrap of scribbles.
A fragment of warmth, California, indolent
sunsets on the beach, a boy beside me,
something unnerving scratched in sand.

Against Overlong Sound Checks

After a few years I'm less afraid, less appalled
by my asymmetry, my out-of-whackness, but
it's hard. I try to stroll past the dreadlocked
neo-hippy coffeehouse loiterers or the ripe-as-
well-oiled-weapons bare-midriffed teenagers
with an air of unconcern, bravado — an absolute

sham. Plus I'm a fool because no one cares.
If anyone stares, it's at my dog, iconoclast
Jack Russell terrier, and then only askance.
The street's distracted, a Gilligan's Island
of thought-castaways, minds dwelling on

misplaced semicolons. "It's a sound check —
get over it," the asinine pseudo rapper whines
in what would have been a serene Saturday
afternoon tavern. Yes, get over it. Everyone's
missing something. Random digits and organs.
Timely legacies. Untroubled pasts. A brain.

ATM

Fluorescent post-midnight idleness,
alone with my thoughts. At my feet,
detritus of the day's transactions, negative
account balances, inadequate pay stubs,
each uncalculated scrap a measure of defeat.
Blessed quiet now after the day's lineup
of charmless mugs and dull fumblers,
plastic intriguingly pliant from trouser heat.
And all so trusting, so organically naive —
most don't even tally the bills! They
never doubt that I am as honest as I seem.
Innocence is a conceit of management — I remark
your cash advances, maxed-out lines of credit,
and glow. That aquamarine smile I cast
into the mordant concrete blackness is one
of machinery, not charity. Take too long
and I'll ingest your card. Yes, I am
exposed, at your convenience, well-lit,
but I am not necessarily open.

Dorothy

Forget the heart, I tell him. *What you've got*
is way better. I fancy the mettle of his metal
between my thighs, red poll of his hatchet
raised high. Nail me in a field of poppies!
Bend me over the emerald throne! *Why*
don't we do it in the yellow brick road?
I croon. We ditch Mr. Scarecrow with
his itch-inducing scruples, picking straws,
and yap-happy Toto won't be watching
me and my tap-dancing pointman, retooled
Sherman tank clanking me to the ground
where we strip and screw, out of our minds
in the fuscous shadows behind the shack,
panting on a bed of tarnished leaves, twigs
ratcheting — Oh he has all I ever imagined,
implements, lubricants, and the inclination
to use them, a deviant tilt. I oil him and he
oils me, hot as a blowtorch under my seersucker,
his tongue a silvery soldering iron, welding
animal to mineral, my mouth grazing his nuts
and bolts. To hell with Kansas, Aunt Em,
gingham. I want to stay with him — to be his.
But he's cool under his tin lid, zippers up
and scoots. To him, it was sport — to me,
salvation. As the balloon wafts, as the munchkins
cavort, as the Wizard faretheewells, I feel
the first stain of rust, my heart's oxidation.

Risotto

Not a good dish for a hot day in June,
arms aching as I stir and stir, one pot
of translucent arborio freckled with onion,
another of simmering broth, the two embracing
before me, both absorption and penetration.
Not the critical heat of the sauté pan, that fire
that sears and seals, but a patient warmth,
steady agitation within which internal structures
are broken down, liquid and grain indulging
each other, the rice yielding its contours readily,
emitting its savoury aromas. A golden congelation
ladled onto plates and partaken *al fresco*, leisurely,
with a glass of Chianti, in the late afternoon shade
of the maple. But that's not all — the leftovers,
once cooled, take shape in your hands, may be
moulded and baked, breaded and fried,
the pleasure in countless permutations.

Refuse (Against Tolstoy)

Imagine Anna Karenina pushing Vronsky away,
a rebuff, saying *it can't be* and walking —
that strong. She feels virtuous, saintly,
spurning a handsome man's advances, unswayed
by flattery, saying *no, never* to the radiance
of *come what may*. Then home to garbage,
her life with Karenin, ironic smirks, stiffness,
a sadness so habitual she's puzzled when a friend
is concerned — *isn't everyone unhappy?* You'll say
she has her son but that's not enough, never is,
Tolstoy knew that. Children are born to leave;
that heartbreak is expected, but the coldness is not.
His apathy, rote responses, back turned.
She finds herself fully aware her thoughts
are unbalanced contemplating stairwells,
balconies, calculating height and descent.
And so the story ends — Anna dead by
her own hand, again, but the man left her
no choice, made her someone who couldn't live
without love, a romantic fiction that angers me —
no woman's that stupid, is she?

Abandon

Bottle of Shiraz on the riverbank, stars
milling overhead like disorderly smokers
outside a lounge, that spilling sense of no future,
violins tuning up, innuendoes about to clash.

I've been unloving for so long, despair
like the hand of God slamming the bar, furious.
I want to swing from the cleft of your chin,
fishtail in your unorthodox arms,

sail up the scalloped stairs to a wine-dark
alcove where nothing remains of the past
but a senescent stain on the carpet.
No shadow of guilt glimpsed in the hall,

no jittery fear of reprisal, no stipulations,
certainly no shame, alcohol eighty-sixing inhibition,
the scaffolds of consciousness dismantled,
degaussed, unhappiness neutralized. Discourse,

not sex, but we cover it all, men, women,
the uncomplicated heat of your leg against mine,
leaning back in upholstery as deep and soft as death
will be when I'm ready for it.

Snow White

Doesn't take long to realize I'm nothing to the prince, deflowered,
gagging at his grim banquet table while he blathers dimly. I say
blah to his chaste caresses, damned castle, scram back to the woods,
to my roughneck miners who like how I sauce their rabbits, spice
their ale. Each morning, I fill seven dinner pails. Bend for seven
sweet kisses at the door, then turn to my chores, regretful. Left
alone too long while they're underground, my bugaboo returns,
a finger of fear like the disfigured hag snagging my brain — I weed
the flower patch, sweep the flagstones, climb a ladder to mend
the thatch, but it's no good. I'm as rattled, as jumpy, as if I cower
under the huntsman's hatchet again, waiting for the end to fall.
I go inside, push their little beds together, cover up and wander
in wanton imagery as I did during that bottomless slumber under glass,
enchantment, visions of sturdy hands, thirsty mouths, hearts pounding
with ferine fervor, digits and organs, too many to count, seven esurient
tongues. Imagine sensible Doc baffled, Bashful asserting himself,
Happy rabid. When they come whistling up the path in twilight,
I'm lost. The things I've been through — assaulted, poisoned, entombed.
I'll do as I wish. A stormy night, no moon. Eight of us round the hearth
with grog; they light their pipes. Doc at my side. I press his palm,
breathless, a hush but penetrating looks. Joy on joy — multiples
of tenderness, an intensity I had not expected. Desire distilled
in their stunted bones. Later, in waning firelight, their muscled
bodies in various states of repose, I mull the unlikely story that led
to this bliss: buckets of diamonds, a windfall of fathers for my son.

Sixteen Years Ago

Wiping the baby's ass, soaping the baby
in the little white tub shaped like a locket,
sequestered on the sofa with the baby,
pinching the nipple into the baby's fierce mouth,
trying to read with the baby in my arms, trying
not to weep when the baby wakes up, yet
loving the baby so much it's like bronze
ringing inside me, impossible to swallow.

Saturday morning. I'm so tired, unshowered,
I ask for help and this time you demur,
It's my day off. Lacking layers, the baby's
raw urgency all over me, I snap back,
When's my day off?
                              Where's your salary?
That's all you said. I was too stunned
to respond. Ridiculous, wasn't it,
to think I could bank on love?

For (Against) Judith

The night after the night you decamped, April's latest repulsive
deluge pulses on the bay windows and a man, drunk I presume,
teeters on my doorstep, howls my address into the muculent dark —
I'm alone, so jittery, gut stitched with your accusations, I call 911,
but he vanishes, harmless, staggering on like someone beaten,
drenched, cell-hailing a cab I think now. The peril I imagined
from him was as illusory, apparently, as my friendship with you.
I'm sorry that I failed to sip coffee after dinner as you wished,
that I'm so unconvivial, abandoning you to your Carol Shields,
your glowering chair, your orphic eyes under your auburn hair,
but I had things to do, homework, baths, scuffing up and down
the stairs for laundry, dishes, every mundane chore *fini* a minor
coup so soon after chemo, a way of saying fuck you, not to you,
Judith, runaway houseguest, but to the one who fucked me, who
waved death in my face like a bloody cape. The boys were hurt
but I explained it was me you detested, not them, that PEI was off,
the school days they would have missed like cold wet shirts to pull
back on. I recycle your malicious missive, left perched on the guest
room pillow like pissed-off cat shit, so calculated to wound, trash
your subsequent self-serving e-mail gasconades, the albino bone
of forgiveness that was in me once gone AWOL, fed up, ducked out
for a pack of smokes while I lay unconscious in the sequestral OR.

Against All That

And the emptiness engendered by it, that absence
between my ribs, a hollowed-out book stuck
on a shelf that I first felt long ago, as a child,
enisled in the outfield, the frost fence playground
where a palsied breeze pawed the cropped dresses
we were forced to wear. *Unfair, unfair,* I said,
weak with dread and certainty that no matter
where I hid despair would find me. So goodbye
to vacuous drunken laughter, unabashed
stripping under stars, goodbye to six-packs on
a charcoal beach, goodbye to hapless kisses,
to being carried out of loser bars, off my rocker
with expansiveness and wonder, with an unhinged
desire to allow, throw the shutters open to dandelions
and daylilies. Goodbye to parties, Janis and Bowie,
to shots in the living room, so long and sayonara
to losing who and where I am, rampant opacity,
hunger and its humiliation, goodbye to low
voices in stairwells, to the indecision of others
when I know what I want, to that fear of regret
that lingers at a table by itself, counting out change.
Once and forever goodbye to regret. To stupidity.
To my father's third wife. And good riddance
to a bald excuse with no more to show than
the red shirt that's wearing thin on its bony hide.

Marie Antoinette's Last Thoughts

I'll say this: every day I learn something new,
such sudden purity, all those hesternal woes
severed, liberated from the grief of the body,
its ridiculous needs. No hands to wring. How
foolish I was in the younger years to succumb
to flattery, blinding myself to the other's narrowness —
I thought he took pleasure in pleasing me — how
foolish also to think of the world as succession,
lines, the autumnal promenade of the spine,
when clearly it's ovoid, haphazard tumbling,
the way time revolves, memory's carousel,
my son laughing, a parfait of images, braided
strands of topaz and gilt. The confection of defeat,
surrender, the shouts of the crowd receding.
They can't touch me, a sinking, weightlessness
and the elation of that, if only it would last,
the embrace, aflame. Why, with such a capacity
for joy, do we choose to create pain?

Tsunami, Earthquake, Hurricane

I check the basement for water eight times a day,
the ceiling for drips, the floorboards for buckling,
and yet sometimes a calm settles over me,
a silence, as if some unconscious generator
switches off and the house stops shivering.
The cessation of artillery exercises at Gagetown.
The cat and dog cohabiting happily. Lately, all we
do is hurt and be hurt, daring each other, divorce
a word that comes easily and hard. *Oh we laugh,*
I say to Madeline, *divorce of the month club.*
But it's no joke. I want to go back to the weekend
before last, how we were equally dismayed
by the poet slash songwriter at the Playhouse,
absconded for a pint at the Joyce and then actual
conversation at the bar — imagine that — affection
like the given-up-for-good ginger cat mincing
home or the blush of technicolour when Dorothy
uncorks Oz, as if the crumbled villages in Pakistan
were resurrected, the tsunami waters exiting
the auditorium in orderly rows, a generation of
orphaned children descending the palms, unharmed.

After Roncesvalles

Wayward, volitant, his fingers skim the scars, the absence
etched on my ribs, knowing it scares me, insisting *yes*
to the *no please* of my gasp as if he were focusing
the aberrant lens of his antique camera on neon at night,
backlit boulevard windows denuded of jewels, conjuring
the memory that I've tried to kill, death's dick up my ass
in the oncologist's office, merciless dossier of statistics
and odds, but recasting it, the way his photos eroticize
orange and purple light, draping fluid fabric over blackness.
I'm grateful, humbled too, since we've veered these last few
years into acidity, provoking each other with hostility
and tears, his belligerence on Roncesvalles, *I can't take this,*
walking away, his body a balled fist of deep-rooted resentment,
incredulous fury, leaving me there, alone on the tucked-in
street, the old world Polish groceries locked, flower stands
deflocked. Then, when I'm sure we're through, the next morning,
tenderness in Union Station, seeing me off, the previous night's
incisive pain healing, not reconciliation per se, but recognition,
stitching our ragged dehiscence into an uneven seam so that
long after we kiss and the train begins its imposition, stirring
out of anaesthesia, I feel his hands all over me still, lambent
as wheels on a track, flanged steel straddling the riveted rail.

Against Coyotes

Bushrats, ambushing unaware housecats, snipers
reconnoitring their Leningrad of suburban sagebrush,
asphalt and gravel, their alto bagatelles infiltrating
late night TV. One worms into my sister's skull,
scratches up a bed of ganglia and whelps a malign
brood there. Another screws me behind the house,
gets me stoned first, then lifts my shirt, lipsticks
my nipples with foam from the creases of his chops.
One dogs my Joan of Arc mother, dragging a leg,
aping her pathos, her someday-my-prince-will-come.
I hate that one. As I do the one who shoots craps
in Vegas with my father, claws clotted with caked-
on lies, snores with him in a parking lot off the strip,
both of them infinitely more at ease in the casino's
cornucopia of tedium, oddballs, than they are at home.
One's here with me now, arthritic, his calcified bones
buckled in the warmth of a folded afghan, sorrow's
psychedelia tickling his siesta. I stroke his skinny
ruff and he shivers with pleasure, his mulligrubs
vanquished, as if he had given discontent a smooch
and a hug, hailed a cab for it, pitiless, turning away.
This one I suffer unto me. With a dagger, I open
his belly, curl into the vaginal grasp of its cavity
and shelter there, sheathed in repudiation's regimentals.

Against Stagnation

Summer's air of unwashed shirts, the river limp
and low as a drifter, its apathetic odour parked
in my epiglottis like heartburn, the sourness
of not caring. Bilge-borne algae, a cowl of larvae
on the drainage ditch's black shoulders, the itchy
omnipresence of indignation sparking a red rash,
repetitive thoughts like a hateful tune in my head,
a dripping tap. Two mallards barking, each convinced
the other's inadequacy is the root of the problem.
The crows rant their frustration. None of us knows
what to want, other than change. Not that cloying
cant of spring's renewal, but destruction, the freshet's
more indiscreet urge to shake things up, purge the rot,
last winter's sordid mess of mistakes, snapped branches,
the inward steaming heap of misplaced passions, one-
sided friendships, two-faced loves. Dump out the over-
stuffed drawers. Make room for new disappointments.

Mrs. Oliver Mellors

What is it now between us, dearest?
Slumped over your tankard, your narrow
back turned. Such a carnal man once,
uncouth, profane — I loved that in you,
how little you cared for the commonwealth,
the two of us desolate, lonely salts lost
in the penetralia of passion, our smut-
blackened hovel. Pub nights, watching
the younger ones pair off, their naive self-
assurance, so dismissive of us, swaggering
like potentates, yet blind, never realizing
it's the old hands who exercise dominion,
sovereigns of the art. After so many years,
a willingness to explore, trawl the unstable
edge, no hesitation. Your tenderness leavened
with mock brutality, a knee between my thighs.
Your unbridled delight. Where did that go?
I'm going out. I can't stand it anymore,
how you retreat within a hood of boredom,
let the sandstorm blow. Once I hated
to leave, dodged appointments, snubbed
allies to be near you, your frank nakedness
under the rough army blanket. Now I'm
going out, out to commune with the horses,
to kick the board walls of ambivalence.

And Now the Looting Begins

Mid-August dinner party, unbeknownst to us, two systems
are trysting in the stratosphere, clandestine, disco bumping
and grinding, so that, as if orchestrated, with Camembert
and black grapes arrayed, glasses filled, we're silenced
by a massive flash, another, freeze frame round-the-circle
eye contact, brief thrill, and the lights expire. As if the house's
heart had stalled. A non-event, as banal as the end of love.
We relax collectively, two blue tapers already lit, appreciating
the unfamiliar silence, no fridge tick-tocking, no Portishead,
no ceiling fan, as we debrief, blackouts of the past recollected
wistfully, like once-troubling liaisons. Over them now. Later,
after everyone has left but my recent ex, a perfectly predictable
occurrence of ex-sex, red wine denouement that I'll regret
tomorrow. But for now, it's pleasant, sated in all respects.

Against Skunks

Not bitter, but acrid, an apocalyptic scent of treachery
and abomination, the just-sprayed dog recoiling indoors,
eyes swollen, vomiting, before I realize, and the stench,
faint at first, that brought me downstairs, jackhammering
my nostrils. I tie the dog outside and hightail to the only
still-open drugstore where my malodorous malady amuses
the late night crew. Then douche the dog with peroxide
and baking soda, the panic receding as I rub and rinse,
thinking the worst is over, stupidly, as it turns out, because
the smell has mushroomed, migrating in the seconds that
the dog was inside through the kitchen and into the upper
floors, corrupting every room. I open windows, aim fans,
wash clothes, sheets, towels, and in the days that follow,
dope the house with air fresheners but the aroma enjoys
an epic longevity, rejuvenating even weeks later, when
the dog swims, pungency leaking from his coat like pain,
the ache that I thought I had neutralized with our separation,
my disavowal of marriage and you, that recurs with every
casual mention of X's name. Duplicity, collusion, it all
comes back, your guilty walks, the selfish daydreaming
lust that I recognized, guilty myself. Again, I'm spitting,
throat constricting, betrayal's rot lingering long past love.

Against Irony

All these long last walks beside the thin-lipped
river, negotiating our separation out of earshot.
We probably look happy, like any self-satisfied
couple, absorbing June's reconstituted warmth.
I know I feel lighthearted at times — *like anvils
lifting off my shoulders*, I tell a friend, to admit
it's over. And we touch occasionally, the way
lovers would, as when I swear to nearly 20 years
of perfect fidelity. Never wanted anyone else.
You grin, hook an arm around me. Remain silent.

Against Marriage

In the aftermath of emotion, last summer's
sundering, solitude becomes the bottle stashed
under cushions, tilted behind cookbooks,
each desperate gulp a balm to salve January's
unspeakable sadness. The nihility that follows
a storm, woozy sun refusing to rouse. Days
dribbled in goblets of bitterness: how stupid
I was, how little it matters, craving that liquor.

Against Scaffolding

The way I'm compelled to dismantle, to bare the walls
beneath the muddle, warmed by the exertion,
like the two men in orange coveralls I'm watching
from the vacant Via station, hours until my train,
minus 30 outside, as they tear down scaffolds. I imagine
their pliant male strength, stately steel singing as it
tumbles, how they shout in the gale. I'm headphoned
and goose-downed, shivering even indoors. Behind me,
a 20-year marriage discomposed, sustained this long
only by self-deception. Ahead, the friendships I'm
dieseling toward have drifted, affections as ephemeral
as ashes. No matter. The deliverance of disencumbering —
separate the accounts, partition the property, bulldoze.
Leave only the concrete subfloor. When I look up,
the workers have decamped, the revamped warehouse
left crouching on its foundation, paint scraped from its eyes.

Against Losing My Wallet

Where we huddled on the curb by the Parkdale LCBO,
booze-famished, gobbling Doritos, house-arrest girl
hustling drinks on the sidewalk behind us, you and I
mooting my elsewhere husband, his ability to carry on
with me, while desiring another. *Easy,* you shrugged,
locking eyes, the meaning of your smile unmistakable.
Stumbled off and left it there. Along with the glare
of your later evasions, my cheesy flashbulb enlightenments,
remembering the supposedly friendly goodbyes you
subverted, that kiss on King, the bus idling astern.
The taxi you hailed, then held me too long in the open
door, the cabbie's gloomy tact. And my complicity.
How willing I was. Yet how much I actually cared.
Other than that and the bowl of noodles house-arrest
girl had on my Visa, I left nothing of value behind.

Against Therapy

Climb down out of the shuddering limbs of worry,
anxious pacing, oddball winter moon peeking
cockeyed through the kitchen window, that mad
vein in your left temple throwing itself against
the wall. Debark. Drop anchor in calmness,
corporeality, the mouth so self-aware, tongue
trying to look casual, sidelong skulking up
against the teeth. Slip down the throat like
squeezing between chairs, a fluid muscularity,
into the entropic warmth of the chest cavity,
pink challis to pull around your shoulders.
Harbour there, alee, the background slap-slap
of the heart masking distraction. Memory's
a stack of cards on the table. A bottle and a glass.
Your father weeping over your sister's embalmed
grimace, gripping your hand. The sombre surgeon,
privately grief-stricken after her third miscarriage,
conveying "suspicious cells" to you as innocuously
as she can. Lunch is definitely off. Steady, steady.
Rein the pulse back to a slow canter. Stroll
the gallery, portraits hung from the rafters,
a blond boy who pressed you against a garage
door so many years ago and you eased down
out of his leaning because you were uncertain,
you didn't know if a kiss was what you needed.

Against Imagination

Shut the door, put the laptop to sleep,
a glass of Cabernet and a book to ease
the jitters. My brain like an overwrought
mongrel, can't leave it alone too long
or it chews the table legs, claws the floor.
Wharton, Austen, anything to banish
magpie thoughts. It's a joke, right?
That we are given the ability to see
what doesn't exist, a future that will
never be, to peer into the darkness
full of doubt and hope only to find
no one leaning in for a kiss, no one
with a bottle of Shiraz to share, no one
lighting a smoke and blowing away
from your face, full of tenderness.

Fathom

Saying one thing, thinking another. Rising
in April, expecting spring's harmony,
river willows greening, dandelion sprouts,
but uncurtaining January, agitation of snow.
Laid low, wanting what doesn't exist.
Stupidly investing unwarranted meaning
in minor occurrences, a laugh in the dark.
Defeat, that nauseating slope, the deep end
spooling downward the day I panic, oddly,
in the pool, lose the ability to swallow, calf
cramping up, heart bucking wildly, wanting
neither to drown nor to cause a scene. Unclench,
untighten, pretend — denial's a way of stroking
through pain, ironing it out. Making it
to the concrete lip of comprehension.
It's better this way, hand over hand
to the ladder, not letting go.

Solitude

Like being fourteen again, the parents gone,
the house empty, Janis and the Full Tilt
Boogie Band cranked up at 8 a.m., no one
sleeping in, no husband, kids, no guilt.
On the other hand, no warmth under covers,
no you to coax with my mouth, succubus,
to screw between e-mail and laundry — is it perverse
to want it both ways? To want freedom and us?
Now it's "Me and Bobby McGee," Joplin
co-opting Kristofferson, tremolo bucking —
I always loved her bravado, that boozy passion
for come what may, for thrills, for mindless fucking,
but not her death. Nothing left to lose.
Or everything. Why are we forced to choose?

Subversion

How does she wake up every day to gloom?
Acrid heat of San Diego, poisonous tedium,
even the trees are lethal — acacia, eucalyptus —
coyotes harassing the bitter, tethered dog.
She shoves the covers back, rubs her eyes,
her daughter beyond disintegration, daily
grind of tube feedings and shit, feedings
and shit, my sister's diminished body
a distillation of life, tied with a sheet
upright in the wheelchair or reclined on
the sofa, rubber beneath her. My mother
as dogged, as sturdy, as serious as Sisyphus
humping his rock, her fear of plots — Communists,
liberals, the Kennedys — her right-wing radio
shows ranting, righteous anger, as if what
is wrong with her world is politics. And
my father, his secret life of Reno, Vegas,
stashed in his pocket like a roll of bills,
puttering on Saturdays, linking green hoses
to water the irrelevant trees.

For My Sister's Brain

Fourteen, my abortive attempt at running away,
fizzled, a dud, one night on the beach, Michele
in tears, wanting her mother, phoning from the 7-11.
Then home. I felt merely ridiculous, betrayed.
The next day, summoned to the room in which
my sister languished, vegetative, her brain cratered
by cancer, I stared, wordless, into the mirrored
closet doors. My mother spoke — probably she asked
what was wrong, why I did it, but I can't remember.
A surreal scene, my mother bathing my sister's
ivory-blue body, a green cloth between the legs,
swabbing the stomach tube, the trach, stretching
the limp limbs ten times. I think now it must have
been a way to shame me. But the lesson was lost.
I had no shame. My sister's brain set me free.
Nothing I could ever do could cause that much pain.

Crux

Even from a distance, idling atop the hill,
our rusty van quaking in November gusts,
I detect the tuck of your brow toward hers,
your goose-down-trussed torso canted just so,
elbows abutted as you and she descend the trail
together, quadruple boots crunching autumn's
crust of desiccate, muddied rubbish of oak and elm.
Just walking her home. Yet how you adjust
your stride to hers, unrushed, *your face flushed*
and the way her grin amplifies your exuberance —
you're buzzed, utterly focused, absorbed in her.
I'm not angry, just a bit crushed. My problem.
Suspicion, a relapse of distrust. If I question
you, you'll sigh, nonplussed, say I'm unjust
and, jesus, aren't you allowed to have friends?
This completely sucks, but I don't hate you.
It's self-disgust. The years in which I chose
not to see, disbelieving distance, indifference.
Time to shift gears, let out the clutch.

For Fidelity

Patrick in Iowa sitting me down, saying *you know he's not
monogamous*. Yes, I know. And knew and gave not a damn,
wanting him, his uncurbed desire, that urgency to penetrate
the perfection of another. And another. Even now, in my
solitude, lusting only for costly face cream, running the speckled
dog on the riverbank, my eyes elsewhere, I think fondly of him,
his beauty, elbowing the bar in Cut Bank, Montana, so many
years ago, the good band with the midget drummer from Havre
playing "Mustang Sally," everyone imbibing, the Keno girl
chatting up railroad workers, the bar owner's hennaed beehive
nodding magisterially among the tables, nothing ahead
but a manageable stumble to the Park Way Motel and,
next day, eggs at the Big Sky Cafe, the élan of our world-class
hangovers and a lonesome highway to Coutts where the bored
border agents dump out our cans of Coors and search us,
unremarkably, for something we told them we never possessed.

Against Being Convenient

The dog might prefer to hunt, but he won't
walk away from the meat in his bowl.

Against Self Negation

Two green chairs from a second-hand store, cartoonish
in their roundness, plump shoulders stuffed with horsehair,
bought and then abandoned in Calgary. *Too big for the truck.*
Ditto my oak desk. But he's not to blame. I acquiesced.
Gave up those things gladly. As I did my blasted,
misbegotten country with its wars and soon-to-be-false
enthusiasms and my tragic mother, who wept on the phone,
convinced of my doom. She was wrong, but not as wrong
as I believed then.

        My bodily integrity, three C-sections
and their concomitant scars, my left breast, two clumps
of cells that would have been fetuses, my self-respect,
drinking myself into inanity with him all those years.
Watching his hockey, reading his books, trying to love
what he loved so that he would love me more.

        And that
not working. In the end, my peace of mind, knowing
that it was over, his transparent nervousness, reticence,
tight grin, and then reading what he wrote to himself
privately (more self-respect lost), how he wanted another
and how he wished he wanted me. And leaving becoming
the only way to get anything back. To rise before dawn
each day to a day given only to coffee and puzzles,
Saturday's lethargy. And wanting him still.

For the Walker

Such wide Africas of stains on his yellow shroud, cryptic,
indecipherable mumblings, a pace that could only be called
shambling, everpresent, on King or Queen or Brunswick,
cockeyed toque too high, you can't miss him, though I
pretend that I do, feign preoccupation as we approach,
the dog and I, unsteadily on the gelid sidewalk, the dog
in his best red boots (for the salt). I wonder, does he see
us, does he think *that dog has better footwear than me?*

You're being a little paranoid, says the 17-year-old,
helpfully, but that's how I am, always imagining that I
have some effect on the world, that those troubling
hugs at the gym mean something. I am mistaken.
Futility's as ephemeral as anything, our well-shod
footprints dissolving in slush, unremarkable, even
to the walker, who, as we do-si-do on the constricted
path, misses not a beat in his monologue, his harangue.

For Fredericton

Bisecting the Anglican's parking lot, the usual trio of dope-smoking
coughers not there, that's good, then past Aura, but I'll get my free-range
eggs later, to Paradise Imports, where my good man John fixes me up
with a pound of Rainforest blend and Jack (the dog) licks a little latte
foam, to Radical Edge where the winter stock's deeply discounted,
Jack morose in the aisles, reminding me of the kids when I lingered
in the linen department on our way to Toys, but nothing calls to me,
no marked-down fleece that will change my life, that's good too, out
onto Queen, past the poker-faced money machine and the latest bistro
incarnation in the old bank building, something wrong about the pressed
tin ceiling, unappetizing aroma of vaults and coins, stretching our six legs,
mine a little woozy from the gym where, this morning, it was one of those
Jimmy Stewart workouts, everyone chatty, communal pain, joking about
death, that guy with the cute bald spot, married, friendly as usual, a hand
on the back of my neck, but I don't mind, I kind of like it, the illusion
of attraction being all I can handle at this point, I mull that over, day-
dream a little, *hmmm a week in bed*, that makes me smile, and then
a girl wants to talk to Jack so we stop and he sniffs the proffered fingers,
but he's nobody's dog unless they have edibles to offer, so on to King,
double back to Aura, where Jack, tied outside, woofs a little *I'm waiting,*
I'm waiting while I browse the herbal teas, nothing new, buy my eggs
and the cashier comes out with a carrot for Jack, drawing the attention
of two runners who stop to talk dogs and a woman from the house kitty-
cornered holds up her Pomeranian, *his name is Sammy Davis Jr.!*
We laugh, then half a block home to my small house that I adore,
both of us sagging with age, and flick on the propane fire, thinking that
I really do wish my ex well, hope that he's seeing someone nice, and
even if the world is replete with lies and liars, diet doctors, dating websites,
even if horses turned out to be mean and stupid, even if young women
still smoke, and I still, sometimes, just want to get hammered,
it's an adequate life, no snipers, after all.

For George Eliot

The way a record used to skip, the stylus stammering,
I got stuck on *Middlemarch*, read and reread it, afraid
to move on, a form of paralysis, my sympathies not
with overwrought Dorothea, an unlikeable heroine,
but with the narrator, that hamstrung voice. I felt
that she spoke to me, a delusion, I know, but, as I
was in the midst of severing connections, that mattered.
With each ending, I turned to the beginning again,
alone in my non-aligned room, and drank litres
of red wine, cognizant that I had to quit that as well,
while the house carried on below me, teenagers coming
and going, slit-eyed under their dark cobra hoods,
housepet conspiracies, dust and sheddings, the king
of passive aggression nursing his Earl Grey, the vacuum
curled submissively at his feet, the oven black
with the ebonized grease of the Christmas turkey and I
don't even deal with that, just close the book and leave.

For Alcohol

Saturday mornings of annihilating regret, banality, trying to remember
what I said or did. Bamboozled, inert. The debris left in the kitchen,
the 10-year-old masticating his cinnamon toast at a table frosted
with bottles. The cold wind under a thin shirt desolation of self-
loathing, weakness, giving in to seduction, suckered by its fictions.
Simply unable to do it anymore, sick of the empties, shrinking as
from the touch of someone unwanted, never puritanical, though,
I hope, nor proselytizing. Craving quiet nights, the antithesis
of conviviality, Edith Wharton, Jane Austen, working it out,
stacking the good days up like saucers, counting them, allowing
a little proudness, getting to the point where I don't really care
that much anymore, a six-pack in the fridge for friends but for me,
it hardly exists, forgiveness after all the unforgivables, the mercy
of detachment, and, eventually, an uncomplicated nostalgia, sans
recrimination, sometimes wishing I could be that again, that slattern
who courted obliteration shamelessly, bitter pleasure in the epiglottis,
a cold pint on a hot deck, chocolate stout from Quebec, windowless
taverns, banquettes and bartenders, airport lounges, plush hotel bars,
the unknown winking at me from a corner booth, yes, I miss that,
the enhancement, the distraction, without wanting it back, loving
it as I do, sincerely, from a smaller house down the road.

For the Coe Slide

(in Baxter State Park, Maine)

Larch woods opening to sheer slate, sun and silence, maybe half
a mile of drop, the mountain's poker face, a joke on us, bare rock
littered with rubble, a few precarious cairns suggesting a route.
No handhold. No foothold. Disaster licking its lips. Gabriel laughs,
*Oh man, one slip and by the time you got to the bottom, you'd just
be a red streak.* Dave says, *Keep your c.g. low.* Backtracking's
not an option, too much trail behind us, another couple of hours to go.
Nothing to do but wade into it, fight the temptation to plant my ass,
refuse to move. Dave descends first, deciphering the stunted vegetation
for traction, a few pliant branches to Tarzan down, then inch across
the slope, *baby steps,* stop and reassess, acclimate. The mountain's
not to blame. We're the fools, out here with nothing but uncertainty,
instability, my nostrils dilated with free-falling fear. Dave sees that
in my eyes, plants a boot in front of me, says, *Put your foot against
mine, it won't move, you'll be safe.* And I do and it doesn't and I am.

For Pigeon Lake

Not the lake, but the blissful drive there, 45 minutes
alone with you, my bare toes up on the dash for air,
you taking the last turn at Calmar too fast, pointing,
there, that's where the pony threw me, then rocking
along the rutted road, gravelled driveway, past the older,
shunned structures, the bat-shitted bunkhouse, outhouse,
to the newer cottage, all plumbed and sided, your mother
preening on the cedar deck, geraniums in clay pots, that
sense of girding as we exited the car, a knot in my gut,
hoping that it would go well. I can almost smell the dryness
of those times, the beauty and tension, crickets and jackdaws,
the cool lake percolating at the edge of the browbeaten lawn.
Happy just to be with you, despite the anxiety, uncertainty,
inevitable altercations, too much beer in the sun. Years later,
after your father's death, your mother's long waning,
the property mouldered, not forgotten entirely, but neglected,
your siblings' focus elsewhere, until it was finally sold.
In someone else's hands now, as am I.

Acknowledgements

Many thanks to the Canada Council and artsnb (New Brunswick Arts Board) for generous support, without which this book would not have been completed.

A number of the poems in this book appeared previously in a limited edition titled *Against*, published in 2007 by Frog Hollow Press. Many thanks to Caryl Wyse Peters, publisher, and Shane Neilson, editor.

The ending of "Decaf" owes a debt to Charlie Smith's poem "The World as Will and Representation" from *Heroin and Other Poems* (New York: W.W. Norton & Co., 2000).

Thanks to the editors of the following magazines in which some of these poems previously appeared: *Arc*, *Event*, *The Fiddlehead*, *Lichen Arts & Letters Preview*, *The Malahat Review*, *Prairie Fire*, and *Queen's Quarterly*.

"Decaf" was selected as a finalist in *Arc*'s 2004 Poem of the Year Contest; won second place in *Prairie Fire*'s Bliss Carman Poetry Competition, January 2005; and was nominated for the 2006 National Magazine Awards by the editors of *Prairie Fire*.

"After Little Italy" was shortlisted for *Prairie Fire*'s Bliss Carman Award, January 2005, and selected as a finalist in *Arc*'s 2005 Poem of the Year Contest.

"Against Sanitation" and "Through" were nominated for the 2006 National Magazine Awards and the Pushcart Prize by the editors of *The Malahat Review*.

"Marie Antoinette's Last Thoughts" was selected as a finalist for the 2007 National Magazine Awards, nominated by the editors of *Queen's Quarterly*.

"Against Therapy" was nominated for the 2008 National Magazine Awards by the editors of *The Fiddlehead*.

"Dorothy" and "Against Coyotes" appeared previously in *I.V. Lounge Nights*, Alex Boyd and Myna Wallin, ed. (Toronto: Tightrope Books, 2008).

"Impending Death of the Cat" appeared previously, in a slightly different version, in *Jailbreaks: 99 Canadian Sonnets*, Zachariah Wells, ed. (Windsor, Ontario: Biblioasis, 2008).

Thanks to Madeline Bassnett and Triny Finlay for Greek food and editorial advice. Thanks to Ross Leckie for editing this manuscript and for being a good friend.

Thanks to D.P. for companionship and mountains.

Love always to Martin, Kelly, Gabriel, and Mark.